IN
THEIR
VOICES

A POETRY CHAPBOOK

By Charlie Becker

Published by Tofu Ink Arts Press. All rights reserved.
Book design by Brian L. Jacobs, Charlie Becker, Glenn B, JLTY Atelier
Cover Image: Charlie Becker
ISBN: 978-1-958661-33-8 (print)
ISBN: 978-1-958661-34-5 (ebook)
www.TOFUINK.com
A member of CLMP

Contents

Acknowledgments ix

The Hair Chair There 1

Before Sight 2

Seattle 3

Oh, Gertrude 4

Mosaics 6

Through Darkness 8

High School Haiku 9

Coming Out 10

Note To Self 11

This Ark 12

Rush Hour 15

My Heroes 16

Last Call 18

Butterbeans Night 20

The Poets 22

My Turn 23

Main Library 24

Mother At 99 26

Sketching Trees 28

Dear Richard 30

Camouflage 33

Still Life 34

In Mary's Light 36

Photo 38

The Secret Life 39

What They Give 40

My Garden 42

Trees And Me 44

Age Wise 46

Portrait 47

Sonnet In Weho 49

Elegy For James 50

Great Are They 52

This Poem 54

Found Family 56

When It Rains 57

The written and spoken words of many LGBT-Q poets and authors have influenced my own poetry since I was a teenager. For this reason, almost daily, I try to read a couple of their poems to find inspiration for my own emerging but yet unwritten lines and verses, coaxing my words to come together as new poems.

Acknowledgments

Versions of some of these poems were previously published in literary journals, anthologies, or books. Thanks to the editors.

Comstock Review: "Through Darkness"

Dandelion Review: "My Heroes"

World Stage Press: Poems in Praise of Libraries, Anthology: "Main Library"

World Stage Press: Friends My Poems Gave Me: "People Who Ride the Bus"; "A Day Made by Mary Oliver"; "Elegy for This Poet"; "The Hair Chair"; "At 100"; "Haiku"; "Rush Hour"; "The Poets"; "Sonnet in WeHo"

A Poem's Medium: "The Art of Seeing"; "There's This Graffiti"; "Mosaics"; "This Ark"

Orchard Street Press: Quiet Diamonds: "Age Wise"

Pigeons on the grass, alas
Pigeons on the grass, alas
Short longer grass short longer longer
Shorter yellow grass. Pigeons
Longer pigeons on the shorter longer
Yellow grass alas pigeons on the grass

Gertrude Stein ("Four Saints in Three Acts")

The Hair Chair There

Where? Once not too far away there lived a woman who grew her hair so long she could braid it into a chair there and sit on it when it was most convenient for her. Wherever she went she had a place to repose relax sometimes blink in an afternoon daydream. Her neighbors then and there became quite envious and tried to buy her hair her chair but she refused even as they threatened to cut her chair her hair while she slept and oh this really scared her. The good old neighborhood seemed like endless unfamiliar faces and smarmy smiles wily eyes ireful ears. There and then she dreamed of lollylob pines stargazer lilies sunbleached swans sipping from her hand and moonlight passing through walls of a copper colored bedroom. When and when she woke she knew she would pack her hair chair into their car and drive out of the city to live by herself in the country alone steering east like a monotonous glass of warm milk until she turned north and careened down and over hills like a San Francisco summer sky and arrived in time to grow a table then a house and perhaps a bicycle.

Before Sight

Echo, echo, echolocation does not need light
to find its way out of darkened winter hunger pangs
it only requires we know how to use bounced sound
tap by tap in the newly whitened phosphorescence
of our wakefulness. Long white cane in hand, flashed sonar
guides us human beings without sight right to the door
demanding to be opened for some cold food or drink
think primary visual cortex with acoustic
locator, no matter, memory and taste enhance
supersede the need for any bright bio-sonic
substitutes, we simply choose sweet, sour, savory
bitter, or umami such pleasures must always come
like waves, incandescent waves, pitched high above the earth

Seattle

rain rain rain rain rain rain rain rain rain rain
rain rain rain rain rain rain rain rain rain rain
rain rain rain rain rain rain rain rain rain rain
rain rain rain rain rain rain rain rain rain rain
rain rain rain rain CLOUD rain rain rain rain
rain rain rain rain rain rain rain rain rain rain
rain rain rain rain rain rain rain rain rain rain
rain rain rain rain rain rain rain rain rain rain
rain rain rain rain rain rain rain rain rain rain
WET

Oh, Gertrude

Rose is
of course
she is
isn't she
Rose
I always thought
she was
just Rose
then
it doesn't matter
to me
a name is just a name is just a name
unless
she changed it
for some other reason
which is totally OK
but now
if she's a Rosie
just Rosie
I mean
I could see that
I guess
no longer Rose
that might work
kind of like
a non-Rose
anymore
or even
Rose-Rose
like a bi-Rose
(stranger things have happened)
because
I will always
think of her
as Rose is

my Rose
good old Rose
except
I wonder
worry a little
if she keeps changing
and changing
which she might
and suppose
she becomes Ross
or something
like that
then what
would I do
until
I guess
I could deal with
would have to deal with
them
mostly, too
my Ross.

Mosaics

I.   Hold my hand
my hand
hold my
and
our hands

II.   when the jacarandas
snow purple
onto grass, cars, sidewalks
we sit
we
at the breakfast window
listen
May gathers itself
in our tiled
Fauvist backyard

III.   hold
with love with

IV.   when the fragrance
of moist leaves
coming figs
wind-shocked tops
of young ochre trees
tells us
spring at last
we walk
we
you and I
outside
on mud vermillion paths

V.   love
with love
is why

VI.   when the quiet spray
of sprinklers
dots air with water
maroon tulips open
informed by straight backs
we with
with love and I
curl my fingers
into your palm
hold hold
close my eyes
promise you
the Milky Way
will be clear yellow
tonight
ocean clouds and stardust
soften its bands
and this is why
we hands
hold
hands with.

Through Darkness

Bio, bio, bioluminescence in essence
gives off light as bright as the first star we see tonight
at heights insightful to the eyes. Luciferase makes
us race like children through dark sparked to capture
fun unspun in forests, fields, near water blinks order
from glass jars just after twilight summers each backyard.
Winged beetles we fly with lanterns in our abdomens.
When mates appear nearby flash back, cast a spell and tell
of life's desire, its own nocturnal, to plant new
and constant offspring in the earth, grant birth glimmering
larvae light-beams, yellow-green releasing energy
free formed shows at our feet complete with magic powers
showering numinous luminous luck, like leap years.

High School Haiku

she was, like, jealous
and he was, like, whatever
so she got, well, pissed

then he was mad back
and she was so over it
that he got real scared

he's, like, I'm sorry
and she's, like, O.K., we're cool
and he's, like, happy

so they, like, went home
and talked all night on smart phones
until, like, they dropped

Coming Out

Gaydar, gaydar, gaydar like sonic human beings
seeing each other for the first time, senses locate
in the dark, at the park, on the streets, between silk sheets
to the beat, where we eat, at the bars, beneath thrilled stars
in the clubs, among found loves, inside shade, twilight's fade
dancing disco, San Francisco come and play, find out
why, modify so freely, get that job, join the mob
scene, dream a clean sweep, take the leap and meet the person
you're meant to be, become your own diverse universe
off the hook, you just choose, nothing to lose come peruse
take some time this climb redefines the lines and then let
nature, nature, nature take its course, all creation
knows the heart from its start finally settles the search

Note To Self

If I could just be good good enough if I could just I could be enough
if just could be enough good if I and good and enough if good were
enough and I
could enough
because even if it's raining and it's going to rain
I know then when it's raining it's going to
rain
until there's enough
good enough
rain
because always enough
is enough
and
longs to be
has to be
good.

This Ark

No, ah no
Noah
did not sit
at home
to isolate
stay safe
no
his genesis
came mid-motion
among the wise
chosen
animals
and we
must travel
like them
surrounded
by the pastel spirit
of our watercolors
see an apricot sun
guide
its tusk-shaped moon
like a friend who longs
to be close
watch the healing
radiate
from dry
tan deserts
to rose-washed
snow tops
follow soulful
vessels powered
by peppermint steam
as they chug and spin
towards nightfall's purple
sky

then wait
then watch
with other curious
creatures
hoping
we, too, will soon
remember
how to be
prolific.

*...at the edge of the city, in the company
of crickets, beside the empty clothesline,
telephone wires, and the moon, tonight
my life is an old friend sitting with me...
Richard Blanco (El Florida Room)*

Rush Hour

Headlights lining boulevards like iced lace
Lexus lovers flashing an orange angst
at Melrose and Fairfax, night-time stares blank.
Hybrids all humming, we plod alongside
each other, windows rolled open to catch
time, claim space. I'm moved by a Mozart mood
on the radio, such an interlude
for my heart and ears, I dream I'm dreaming

yet I raise the volume and start to sing
loud, filling my Prius with turquoise stars
then yellow gold ones falling from on high
above a common voice, twinkled rapture
celesta musical notes now captured
while cars around me burst into applause.

My Heroes

I wanted biceps, big like yours
with a hula girl tattoo
who danced when I flexed
and mighty forearms of steel
real threats to the bullies
who chased and taunted me.
I wanted your strength
your rich, green spinach, I'd watch
you squeeze open the can
with your bare, macho hand
swallow it all in one gulp
and then take Brutus down
without sweating a drop
or losing your gritty grin
scratchy manly chuckle.
I wanted your punch, Popeye, I needed
you to teach me self-defense
I longed to be your forever buddy.

Puff, too, he lived by the sea
and did magic tricks for little boys
the way dragons can, we
fearless frolicked in the autumn mist
best friends and sailed free on billowed
boats far from taunts or cuts of mean kids
who didn't care for fantasy fun or innocence.
I needed you, Puff, your spiked tail
your commanding roar
for myself every time I left home
thinking I was all alone.

Sure, I lived the life of Superman
long before I knew Clark Kent
me growing into a secret
not a bird, not a plane
steeling my face, hiding

what no superpower
could fix or overcome.
I needed you, Superman
your rock-square chin
smiling sureness
each day as my world where cowboys
fell in love with other cowboys
seemed in danger of being crushed.
But in the end, I found you
mortal, imperfect Fred Rogers
me, hopelessly fearful
like Daniel Striped Tiger
wondering where my next breath
would ever come from, Mr. Rogers
you welcomed me into your neighborhood
looked me in the eye and said
I made your day a special one
just by being me.
I put on Fred's cardigan
wore his navy Keds
and took from him a voice
softly sincere, for my own use
the way a real hero
simply must
to soothe
the world.

Last Call

When you enter Orlando
you feel the flutter
of fifty angels overhead
throbbing
the way they do
in heaven

when you drive
the way they do
in Orlando
you sense
the lives of fifty dancers
hovering
around green palm trees
the way free mourning doves do
before they fly away

when you drift
into the silence of Orlando
the way we do
in other people's shadows
you find the words
to speak for those
who no longer can.

In Orlando, late one night
midway through a mix
at the beginnings of their lives
they wanted only to be
someone special
spinning light
fine rhymed designs
lined with steps to crystal stairs
and supposed proposals
bright as rhinestones
under strobes

they wanted years
holy poses
chosen choices
voices fit for lifetimes
laying ground for sounds
of personal soaring.
And, oh, to be
remembered
we must bring them
home-grown roses
handmade
mimosas toasting
gay lives matter
all lives like beatitudes
flattering us
who evolve and gather.
Each day
we must dance
the way they did in Orlando
reflecting their spirits
and then twirling
swirling
unfurling their names
again and again
to heal
memories
and the ones
who always
love them
the way we do
from this side
of the dance floor.

Butterbeans Night

Truckstop off the 10
just outside Sidell
shouting distance to New Orleans
I'm working to be a woman
who drives produce
interstate
I freshen my lip gloss
and check in the rearview
mirror
for rogue whiskers
wrinkles around my shadowed
eyes
and then
tuck
it
into its nebulous
nameless
space deep inside
my skinny
jeans
my smile still staring
back
for the me
I see
who has left
the savage of Texas
behind
and hopes
drives
for a Creole drawl
of the Big Easy
easy
easier for me
my new me
at least
I pray
where
I can pretend
life is more fair
and I belong.

Tonight it will be
butterbeans at my favorite
truck stop
supper for one
with homemade biscuits
savory gravy
I want to become
a regular
welcome
not so afraid
and liked by everyone
as I stride
to a booth
and nod
a hungry group
greeting.
Just then
Gentilly-colored
shadows cross
my skin
as I take off the baseball cap
shake out my hair
and wait
until
yes
there she is
and she comes
to sit
across from me
pad in rough
calloused hand
pencil behind one shiny
pierced ear
tickled by whisps
of straight
black
hair
and reminds me
this time
dessert
is on her.

The Poets

We wash the car on Saturdays, laundry on Monday.
We fold underwear in triangles, white socks into tight balls.
Towels are stacked square, put away.
We harvest tomatoes in the north yard, roses facing west.
In between we leaf through magazines, study recipes, and assume it's
all true.
We choose a car for its shape, broccoli because it's green.
We recycle and stay out of the sun. This is who we are.
Our lives fit into a backpack with our lunches.
We wander through the neighborhood and read in the bathtub.
We look more familiar. We shrink and grow older.
Our friends drink more, forget more, laugh more.
We attend matinees, use a cane, speak of doctors.
We downsize and simplify, visit, reminisce, and move on.
We hibernate, relocate and redecorate.
We hurry to arrive and hurry to leave.
Then we start to write as if we're the lucky ones
who can plant and grow words together the way
morning glories cover green garden fences.
Our writing gives the texture of our skin
carries trees and tastes of fresh jalapenos.
We become enraptured by gemstones inventing comets
pushing our verses to leap into each stellar expedition.
Because all along we have longed for unexpected rhymes
like children who wait by windows to see first snow
and for our poems to speak freely into silent, astonished
spaces long after everyone else has stopped talking.

My Turn

Hands gone wrinkled, skin paper thin, transparent
voice vibrates weak across hairless skull. I have kept my promise
raising your names each day, holding memories inside a breath
who will speak of you when I'm gone

voice vibrates weak across hairless skull. I have kept my promise
the men I lost hardest to AIDS
who will speak of you when I'm gone
Loren, Nick, Kevin, George, Russell, Kim

the men I lost hardest to AIDS
partner, best friends, neighbors
Loren, Nick, Kevin, George, Russell, Kim
longed to go with you, not knowing what else to do

partner, best friends, neighbors
today we're finally together again
longed to go with you, not knowing what else to do
I wrote death poems, prayer after prayer, at your bedsides

today we're finally together again
sitting in a soft chair, frail, drifting, spirited
I wrote death poems, prayer after prayer, at your bedsides
this one is for me, out of breath, out of time

sitting in a soft chair, frail, drifting, spirited
hands gone wrinkled, skin paper thin, transparent
I wrote death poems, prayer after prayer at your bedsides
who will speak of me when I'm gone?

Main Library

A poem has been stalking me
all day
kind of like anger
with bad intentions
and even though I'm over it
how can I somehow use it?

We decide to walk together
into our downtown library
on 5th Street
and I hiss a whisper,
"Look around
all these words
found a place
to live
can't you cooperate
and fit in here somewhere?"

Silent
we sit at a long table
and just doodle for a while
mumble threats
jot syllables
here, there
until I confess first
how lately
I've been unable to write
anything except endings
you know
like a librarian
banning books
he always hoped to share.
I choke a laugh saying
maybe we both
or all of us
need help

these days
imagining a future.

Staring each other down
we make a promise
then and there
to come clean, be respectful
as we really should
in such a holy place
like this central branch
surrounded by wisdom
and the soulful sighs
of book keepers.
Because we both
have come to understand
the most evolved poem
we'll ever meet
will likely be waiting
earmarked
in these stacks
someday
knowing all it needs
is a friend
to read its stanzas
out loud
and grace will follow.

Mother At 99

I don't know why
the mottled ducklings
matter so much today
down preening
after their swim
and my mother rests
amazed by such nonchalance
keeping us rapt
in the other world
of instinct.

I don't know why
I used to hurry
everywhere
busying myself
but now
my father gone
mother asking me why
she's still around
I realize there's nothing else
to do but be
nowhere else to go
but here
and ducks
with eyes to see sideways
as they waddle
not looking ahead
or back where they've been
but only where they are
right now
living fully in their moment.

I don't know why
my mother can remember
wild ducks flying south
from her Watkins Glen childhood

yet she cannot recall
what we had for lunch today
or which room she'll find her bed.
Still, instinct
from her wheelchair
continues to tell mom
to fly
in the most migratory
daydreams
jet-streamed
fantasies of flight
sun and star-gazed leaps
across horizons
patterning prayerful
movements
marking season's end
or beginning
as she longs
to know why
and play out
whatever is next
yet must wait
for my father
or fate
to guide her
landing.

Sketching Trees

There aren't any words left
all of them said or too pure
to think onto paper
and I only feel syllables
as an ache snaking
upwards towards
my mossy trunk, weary limbs
each leaf a riot of sorrows
where at my feet
scrim gloss raindrops
splash to the gloaming
start a winnowing
summon a childhood again
before it's too late.

My searching leads to a pencil
with potential to be dark
enough yet erasable, I am
always like that
growing sideways
filling in
shading new branches
gray as if green
surfaces layered
where bark protects
my thin-skinned self
and helps me breathe.
Roots scumble above
or below ground
all night
and there are secrets
when they comingle
overlap
share water or tell stories
while I crosshatch bumps
of truly adapted growth.

Remember.
I am among
old friends here
gathered and discovered
recycled pad in hand
waiting to be used
for art
because trees have
their way of tracing
and embracing
lacing and remaking us
with their stoic poses
drawing in light
drawing out awe
drawing me to pastels
sketching in mosaics
water coloring daylight
and printing
always imprinting
and at last
archiving.

Dear Richard

I want to be the one
who invites you to dinner
then lights two candles
the one who
puts the spoons next to their knives
centers plates
and slowly folds the napkins
I want to be the one
who offers you a chair
touches your back and smiles
the one who speaks of gardens
grows tulips and gladiolas
and then becomes quiet enough
like sunlit spring azaleas bringing
charity with handpicked bouquets.
I want to be the one who whispers
about healed health and easy breaths
where they hide and must abide.

Life stuns, you know, when it suddenly
does what we couldn't imagine
taking away, ending, starting again
with changed landscapes.
Today we are lucky as we quietly
fold laundry, make a sandwich
walk arm in arm from room to room
and share.
I am the one who sees a new moon
cupped between clouds and expects
you will always know the safety
of camellia petals beneath palm trees
scattered showers of pollen
steel gray hillsides edged with brush
among winter dry
night's first coolness

through open windows
sparkling specks of sundown
and faithful worker bees
who crawl inside the mouths
of roses ready to teach us
what will happen next.

*...This is the first, the wildest, and the wisest thing
I know: that the soul exists and is built entirely
out of attentiveness.*

Mary Oliver (Evidence)

Camouflage

Daily we took walks avoiding each other's space
anticipating.

A year came and went four seasons but no desire
to know the day's name.

We stayed together sometimes hardly saying words
a rigid needing.

Under your face mask I knew you were holding breaths
hoping for cured air.

The holy vaccine finally came and found us
our bodies thawed.

You and I bonded this love as unlikely as
wood ducks and screech owls.

Still Life

My 12-Step friends
tell me to expect
a miracle.
I see
a window frame
one naval orange
baked marble bread
on a picnic table
a white tablecloth
with oval placemats
sunlight silvering
nearby pine needles
and their branches.
I remind myself
be still
life
can be like this
if I hover
over my own small body
watching the heart beat
looking at its own
dimensions and colors
smiling at the hope
it has
hanging on
like the scent of a candle
burning too quickly
too efficiently.

What I have to say is
it's difficult
staying present
these days
when so many parts of me
are detaching
falling into disrepair
yet all around
there are
waking, walking

animals
who breathe and live
without thinking
about anything
other than
feeding their hungers.
Awareness tells them
life is layered
with problems to solve
and jokes to laugh at.
It's that simple
but not easy.

For me
nothing turned out
as I expected.
In my old age
I finally realize
I am not here
to impress
or control
anyone
anything
no
I am here
to learn
to give love
to receive love
and to be dazzled
by what dazzles
along the way
like the miracle
of knowing
I am human
which means
I am glowingly
imperfect
wildly
free.

In Mary's Light

At 6 A.M. an artful armadillo
grunts across the patio, his
padded footprints echo
in the morning moonlight, birds
rustle trees, crickets scratch
and scrape in mowed grass
as silver layers of sunrise wake
the room. We wait in bed. Life
seems harder now, more harsh
landscapes look the same
but clouds and air around us
sit stormy cautious yellow
while we learn to anticipate
take shallow breaths on a rainy day.
We stay where we are and worry
some more, wondering what caused
this uncommon bad weather.

Believers turn now to Mary Oliver
poems because she knows
we do not have to be good.
If wild geese leave pencils
on her tree branches, then raindrops
can be like comets, free beacon
particles streaming into puddles
the earth will welcome and absorb
into itself. We Angelenos have learned
to live with bumper to bumper sunny
skies, endless light-filled afternoons
blue like swimming pools, traffic-jammed
waves of heat blinding as bliss.
We are all spoiled children
tanned eternally at play on the outside
fixed inside with excess sun and vitamin D.
Streets high in Hollywood have such power

get covered with red carpet, they stand
alone as rainfall-free zones.

By midday, Mary takes over and guides us
around our city where rain comes steady
but we are no longer afraid of getting wet.
Brooks trickling with ideas gurgle
at the curbs, dogs shake off the fur
of their discontent, palm fronds shine slick
grass and impatiens blink their eyes
in the light, thirsts quenched, wild
songbirds leave nests and chirp
as they twirl, bathe away months
of dusty mites, and we, like school
kids, can jump, slip and splash
drenching our new shoes.

Photo

You love me
too much
I suspect
you there
breathless
taking
my picture
while I fight-or-flight
pose
shy
slightly vain
you see it
in my doe eyes
and the flirtatious
lift of my leg
of course
that's all surface
on the outside
until the stillness
of life's façade
by summer trees
matters
and a woodsy green
drawn from inside
is like the desired lightness
about a cottage
then
I need to warn you
once again
how my wild
always happens
when I silently
summon my hind muscles
and exhale
to affirm
with detached grace
in the next instant
I will choose
to run.

The Secret Life

of cottonwoods and willows
oaks among us
in the groves
of maples next to evergreens
grass and moss at their feet
of chestnuts and apples
reflecting back
moonlight
crepe myrtles and pines
glancing at a harvest
of loneliness
neediness
in the midst
of camellias and magnolias
bright flowers
along exposed roots
of birches and beeches
wishes, skies, and dreams
of palms
such as mine
who dread the darkness
and cold
talking to themselves
longing for summer's casual
conversations
outside
and I wonder
if trees feel
abandoned
whenever
others
go inside
and close
the door.

What They Give

First there is the lanterned
prodding
of twilight
then the symmetrical curl
of leaves unfurling
those brushed whispers
shushing and hushing all desire
to walk
or touch
another living thing
my trees
by nature are generous
tending and bending
taking light
returning shade
conserving water
later sweating
saps, seeds, fruit
with shared breaths
like embraces
overlapping limbs
in the warm familiar
of internal Zen
they nightly create.
I have never felt
lonely
walking in this forest
searching a life
outside
my bedroom window
the comfortable
steady stillness
and roots claiming place
belonging
in a way I want

deep inside myself.
Consider our conversations
emerald crown to earth
concentric rings settling
trunks
becoming networks
shaping kinships
like lifelines to offspring
because
we have learned
to grow
in darkness
drop leaflets
set buds
feed awe
to surrounding wildlife
while we wait
hands exploring bark
as if it were
ancient Braille
longing to be
spoken
in the vigilant
morning blush
of our hunger.

My Garden

Each morning
I go outside
and visit my hydrangeas
the roses, mums, and bees knees
I know they wait
for my essence
as they lean toward me
showering in my praises
whispered thanks
for their leaves and flowers
wild colors
I live
to gently touch
the air around them
like we're family
or old friends
who I must protect
from nature's daily need
to renovate.

Today
I foresee
the same for us
and whisper my hopes
about more beauty
more art
anything we might create
grow
together
and give back
to be enchantingly
lasting
everything
we do
that might be good

enough
to surprise
always teaching us
how to recognize
and like
exactly
who we are
among the carefully planned
chaos.

Trees And Me

Harmless
we talk to ourselves
at night
even though we're surrounded
by others
we wonder
what's on the sky's
other side
when daylight seems
most unlikely
I do often
question
why I'm not
majestic
never quiet stand
proud or tall
and neighborhoods know me
by this posture
slow stride
saved footprints
among foliage
searching for home.

Innocent
we ask ourselves
if it will hurt
when leaves are torn
from our branches
will we cry out
to those
who have witnessed
even the gentle hands of a woman
or roughness
of a hurried, unfeeling man
can we heal

when given
more light
and will it ever
be enough
to just listen
for the plaintive call
of geese
from a comfortable
weathering distance.

Age Wise

I always thought
there was something
to win
a silver cup
golden handshake
royalty nod
first prize
an overwhelming
beautiful
action
I was supposed to take
as an artist
or do-gooder
but when old
finally came singing
and vernal pooling
it gave me
permission
to simply
wonder
how many more
hugs from friends
how much more love
into my hands
and the number
of times
I would
blow out
all the candles
with one breath
because
even as a child
I constantly wanted
to know just how high
the highest
I was ever
going
to be able
to count.

Portrait

sleeping, leaves and stems lean into darkness
a graceful group pose, heavier, more dense
while photosynthesis remembers
ancestors being worshipped and adored

a graceful group pose, heavier, more dense
creates sudden silent enchantment for me
ancestors being worshipped and adored
illuminated as powerful lives

creates sudden silent enchantment for me
apprehending beauty and its wisdom
illuminated as powerful lives
now our symbol for the eternal

apprehending beauty and its wisdom
I commune, pilgrim in the mystery
now our symbol for the eternal
each forest becomes a monastery

I commune, pilgrim in the mystery
hours pass, work continues underground
each forest becomes a monastery
roots growing extensively as branches

hours pass, work continues underground
and above, sap inside each memory
roots growing extensively as branches
an appeal so deep it speaks for itself

and above, sap inside each memory
trees, like art, need not be anything else
an appeal so deep it speaks for itself
sleeping, leaves and stems lean into darkness

Let this be my only solace
Just to know you love me so
(James Baldwin, Paradise)

Sonnet In Weho

Just sayin' I'm reppin' my gayborhood
girly he-men, burly grannies, all good.
Yo, bro bitches givin' me shade, we hood
we should be tight, right? Fool, you know gays rule
don't be hatin', segregatin' that's cruel.
You got two mommas and two poppas, beau
sing it, free your diva and bring it, ho
we all together, the best way to go.

And now, world, we down with the swirl, slag fag
I mean, my street, old news, mad hags, glad drags
no jive, take the drive. Twinks, tweekers, porn mags
boy toys, queens of the hive, way full of scorn
on the horn, slow down, don't be crazy torn
lose the fear, we be livin' it, reborn.

Elegy For James

I used to think love
was all about the opera
barbed wire and battlefields
prisoners and mistaken
midnight
madnesses
the wins with losses
and heartfelt arias
but now as I read
by the light of his poems
he writes with love
the love is light
I see
love
is more than
my controlled
snowflakes covering
almond orchards
late in springtime
blackbirds
swooping down to land
on streetlamps
just at dusk
sodden Iowa
soy fields startled by summer's
rolled-up sleeves eager
to plow
tulips blooming
by the thousand
free of shadows
living for their own
relentless colors
or innocence
innocent in bed
swearing
to always tell the truth.

No
love
is more
to him
true love is
the only reality
its own terror
the only hope
and the grateful
knowing
he was seen by another
for his truest self.

Lucky for us
today
his poems
never die
even as
he lays
in a grave
from where
his written words
grow
stronger, larger, louder
while his poems
bemuse, sooth, refuse
death
singing
unsung stanzas.
Isn't this how
all poets spread
love
by speaking
through their sleep
surrounded by afterlife
eternal as a constellation?

Great Are They

Unkept promises taste
like undercooked words
as they leave the mouth
and ricochet off of sidewalks
in America
freedom comes to some
but not all
brothers and sisters
it's like playing a board game
fixed
in favor of wealthy white
males
weighted on their side
of the scales
everyone else illegal
subject to arrest
victim to attest
to public shaming
we must seek to give
salvation to ourselves.

Great are they, great are they
who sing for justice
Great are they great are they
who fight for freedom

Today we leave all self-sabotage
needing no outside forgiveness
our love is the beginning
of a kiss to confirm
a revolution
against an institution
church and state
love and hate
black and white
I mean men kissing men
women kissing women
no longer hiding
in shadows of fear.

Great are they, great are they
who sing for justice
great are they, great are they
who fight for freedom.

The day comes now
to the streets
straight white male
supremacy crushed
under our feet
kicked in the mouth
by our words
shoe after unlaced boot
and their teeth
like free-thrown dice
splintered in the roll.
Why
why do they try
to deny
my civil rights
and claim fame
for themselves
without blame,
why
why do they try
to oppress me
if my heart's desire
is another man
or someone of a different
skin?
The power they hope to win
is an illusion
so let's bring this to a conclusion:
No matter how long
it takes
or the course it snakes
their wrongs
will never undo
my rights.

This Poem

There's this poem
for all of us
it beams in the dark, sparks remarks
parts of speech packed and stacked
vowel to vowel, pleas to howls
chants and rants, proposes, it noses its way
across our skin and then sings, grows wings
flings whole words against the wall until they submit
fit, witness our lives
round rhymes, lined verse, you know
it has hands, makes plans, stands alone
shown shimmerings of what metaphors can do
we wait for it, shake for it, hate for it to end.

There's this poem
here
hanging in the air
like a scent of holy Roman candles
or an aroma of bones
known in catacombs for years composing space
laced ceiling to floor with nouns
knelt in prayer there, kings' long fingers
wearing rings, golden things
bringing bejeweled language
to our mouths.

There's this poem
see
it has eyes and cries for friends
who died too young, too soon
before they knew what poets can do.
If it took a village to raise us poets
then I say it takes our words
to raise us up:
The ones who were oppressed but still
spoke the truth, the ones who wrote

in secret, silent journals
or shouted out into empty rooms, the ones
who scribbled onto sides of buildings
or protest signs never to know their manifesto
unfold, the ones shot down by guns or AIDS
as they prayed for healing, the ones
who were our loves, the ones who hoped
to reach landings, turn corners
and find the crystal stair
there
there
there's this poem.

Found Family

Unbow your head, get off your wounds and knees
eyes open, unborrow time
and lift your shoulders back, unclasp
worried fingers, stretch them tall
like giant redwoods do, expose those long lines
of your palms to air and loud your voice
strong each word, inhale what's done
about your past but exhale into the future.
The lies you told yourself in childhood
already afraid of what was coming
were never true, you were nothing bad
only good, you were nothing wrong
only right, there was just your nature
there was simply your heart
and the deepest sense of knowing.

So tell me now you're coming out
and I will cry with you, your storied silences
cowerings in corners and dependence
on gray areas, self-denying pleas
forced apologies, half-lived dreams
and censored visions.
You will know a world of possibilities
soon
inclusion, infusion, communion
people who get you and speak
your lifestyle, you will feel
befriended, revived, recreated.
Unbow your head
get off your knees and wounds
then just move
towards traced footsteps of our ancestors
found-family elders
who can teach you
how to recognize and fill
custom-fitted ruby slippers
with your own true purpose.

When It Rains

Where do unhoused people
go
when it's raining
storms start
pelting their back
and front
doors
penetrating
cold and wet
their park benches
empty
sidewalks soaked
tell me, please
where do unhoused children
go
when it rains
so hard
winds pushing water
into shoes
eyes shadowing
into slits
schools closed
churches locked
let me know, alright
where do unhoused mothers
go
when the rains arrive
darkness too early
hunger too deep
shelters full
hospitals overcome
I wish I knew
because
at night
charity freezes

faith falters
even as the ground becomes
a river
and washes away
because
where will we all
go
when a season
brings downpours
of misfortune
and losses
because
when it's raining
I miss my friends
outside CVS
sharing a sandwich
or bags of Cheetos
spare change
I try to give them
tell them
hope
their lives will turn
around
find a way
we talk about
health and being
sober
social services
and plans
to shower under
warm water
at the LGBT Center
I try to give them
tell them
about my other friends
and me
our 12-Step meetings

that surely saved
us from the bullies
of the world
and ourselves
because
when it rains
I want
I
want
so badly
to stay
in bed
cycs closcd
and just listen
listen to warm
sounds of comfort
knowing
for today
we're safe
finally holding
close
the shape
of our relentless
desire
to just
be.

Charlie Becker writes poems about art and arbors, friendships and fauna, weather and witnessing. Some of his poetry has been published in the following journals: The Comstock Review, Passager Journal, The Dandelion Review, Tofu Ink Arts Press, and Quiet Diamonds (Orchard Street Press). His first chapbook, *A Poem's Medium*, was also published by Orchard Street Press in 2022. His second chapbook, *Dodging Bullies*, was published by Finishing Line Press in 2023. Charlie is a retired speech and language specialist and presently lives in Laguna Woods, California, with his partner, Aubry.